BUSTA RHYME

I SHUFFLE THROUGH MY MIND
TO SEE IF I CAN FIND
THE WORDS I LEFT BEHIND
- GREEN DAY

HAMPSHIRE

Edited By Donna Samworth

First published in Great Britain in 2017 by:

Coltsfoot Drive
Peterborough
PE2 9BF
Telephone: 01733 890066
Website: www.youngwriters.co.uk

All Rights Reserved
Book Design by Ashley Janson
© Copyright Contributors 2016
SB ISBN 978-1-78624-832-9
Printed and bound in the UK by BookPrintingUK
Website: www.bookprintinguk.com
YB0301Q

FOREWORD

Welcome, Reader!

For Young Writers' latest competition, *Busta Rhyme*, we gave secondary school pupils nationwide the challenge of writing a poem.

They were given the option of choosing a restrictive poetic technique, or to choose any poetic style of their choice. They rose to the challenge magnificently, with young writers up and down the country displaying their poetic flair.

I am therefore proud to present *Busta Rhyme - Hampshire,* a collection that's packed full of verse that offers a unique glimpse into our younger generation's thoughts and feelings; from what their concerns are and where their dreams lie, whether it's from a love a football, to the harshness of a war-torn world, or from heartfelt issues or society in general, this compilation features it all.

Here at Young Writers our aim is to encourage creativity in the next generation and to inspire a love of the written word, so it's great to get such an amazing response, with some absolutely fantastic poems.

Finally, I hope you find the poems that lie within these pages just as entertaining as I did and I hope it is kept as a keepsake for many years to come.

Donna Samworth

CONTENTS

Ash Manor School, Aldershot

Maddie Jenkins Woodford (11)	1
Heather Dunsmore (11)	2
William Wedgwood (11)	4
Kai Jepson (12)	5
William Fanthorpe (11)	6
Holly Andrews (11)	7
Tyler Lyons (11)	8
Oliver Hamer (12)	9
Maddy Williams (11)	10
Emily Rose (11)	11
Chloe Evans (11)	12
Alfie Drake (11)	13
Swasti Sharma (11)	14
Daniel Westcott (12)	15
Liona Platford (11)	16
Khushi Limbu (13)	17
Daniel Bunce (11)	18
Alexander Stephen Turner (11)	19
Daniel Hebberd (12)	20
Hollie Eaton (12)	21
Niamh McFadden (12)	22
Sian Gillingham (13)	23
Jess Peacock (11)	24
Sasha Marie Garratt (12)	25
Courtney Sivyer (11)	26
Leanne Matthews (11)	27
Kristina Allyson Ecclefield-Walton (12)	28
Cerys Trafford (11)	29
Niamh Wilson (11)	30
Billy Dong (13)	31
Iosto Iacomelli (11)	32
Emma Chapman (11)	33
Joshua Lytton (11)	34

Bridgemary School, Gosport

Freya Eve Kinlough (13)	35
Hannah Graham (13)	36
Liberty Kappa (14)	38
Luke Tunstall (14)	40
Crystal Frampton (14)	42
Livia Giles (14)	44
Hannah Childs (14)	46
Brett Reynolds-James (11)	47
Serena Jane Day (13)	48
Harvey Ayling (13)	49
Jack McEwan (14)	50
Millie Edney (14)	51
Keira Garrett (11)	52
Callie Moore (15)	53
Lewis Walker (14)	54
Tyrone Martin-Menditta (13)	55
Lee Brown (15)	56
Ellie Moore (12)	57
Rhys Lewis (12)	58
Sommer Moore (14)	59

Brockwood Park School, Alresford

Rowan Males (16)	60

Charter Academy, Southsea

Yasmin Sirokh (11)	61
Sabrina Victoria Robson Thompson (12)	62
Haseena Rahimi (11)	63
Poppy Edwards (13)	64
Lily Drennan (12)	65
Jack Drennan (12)	66

Frankie Wall (12)	67
Jasmine Alicia Smith (13)	68
Natasha Spree-Ashdown (13)	69
Dylan Wilding (12)	70
Daisy-Nell Tupper (12)	71
Christopher Barker (11)	72
Ethan Newton (12)	73
Humayra Elme Ali (12)	74
Hana Tvardkova (12)	75
Poppy Cartwright (11)	76

Regents Park Community College, Southampton

Robyn Langston (13)	77
Heaven-Leigh Monces (14)	78
Edie Smith (14)	81
Aimee Hollie-Jean Cartmel (13)	82
Isabella Richardson (13)	84
Mia Breedon (14)	86
Olivia Ebbutt (15)	88
Luke Day (13)	90
Patryk Mikietinski (15)	91
Jaymie Stevens (15)	92
Nathan Hill (13)	93
Mishel Mathew (14)	94
Emily Grace Fraser (13)	95
Malika Chentoufi (13)	96
Angel Freeman (14)	97
Madi Bennett (13)	98
Alisha Danielle Hooper (15)	99
Cora Byrne (13)	100
Ajit Digwa (15)	101
Evelyn Lexie Pybus (13)	102
Minshana Muneer (14)	103
Phoebe Harris (13)	104
Szarida Ciwinska (13)	105
Jake Barry (14)	106
Aleksandra Koperkiewicz (15)	107
Robyn Caine (13)	108
Emily McLachlan (13)	109
Sam Bowyer (13)	110
Ajaypal Singh (13)	111
Liam Kennedy (14)	112

St George Catholic College, Southampton

Stephane Yonga (14)	113
Olivia Wakely (11)	114
Yulu Chen (12)	116
Oluwatitofunmi Euler-Ajayi (11)	117
Erin Brady (11)	118
Martin Shumba Mulenga (12)	119
Natalia Spyt (11)	120
Molly Barker (11)	121
Daniel Hamidy (11)	122
Mehrab Choudhury (11)	123
Philip Wilk (11)	124
Wiktoria Krupa (11)	125
Michalina Wielgosz (11)	126
Ethan Marston (11) & Ellie	127
Luke Hooper (11)	128
Jowan Healey (11)	129
Roman Allen (11)	130
Daniel Sebastian Koch (11)	131
Charlie Wright (11)	132
Abi Ogunleye (11)	133
Dann Lacea (11)	134
Akbar Majid (11)	135
Zhiyong You (11)	136
Olivia Proud (11)	137
Samuel O'Callaghan (11)	138

The Connaught School, Aldershot

Landing Badjie (15)	139
Nicholas Jarrett	140

The Portsmouth Academy, Portsmouth

Isabella Stapley	142
Rheanna North (14)	145
Lilly-Rose Adams (13)	146
Chanice Stevens	148
Kya Athena Patrick (14)	149
Kitty Lydford	150
Macy-Mae Jenkins (13)	151

Tasnim Ahmed (13) 152
Caitlin-Rose Goode 153
Mia Marner (14) 154

Wildern School, Southampton

Chloe Headland (15) 155
Madeline Bendell (11) 156
Esme Thompsett (12) 157
Elizabeth Pugh (11) 158
Victoria Anne de Bruijn (11) 160
Tia Lucking (12) 161
Robyn Harfield (12) 162
Mia Gregory (12) 163
Katie Ridout (11) 164

THE POEMS

The News

In the news today
Clowns were spotted roaming the freeway
These crazy cranksters
Who are just like gangsters
Stir in the dark of night
Tying to cause an artificial fright

In the news today
Trump and Clinton have had an affray
They debate it out, for who has the last shout
To become the president of the USA

In the news today
Hurricane Matt sweeps through like a bomb to crystal display
As it tears through structures
It finds magnetic conductors
As the storm is descending
The city is in need of mending

In the news today
The Galaxy 7 is needing an X-ray
The spontaneous ignition
Is a curious mission
Of why the exploding batteries are all being sent back to the factories

In the news today...

Maddie Jenkins Woodford (11)
Ash Manor School, Aldershot

Addiction

No one can tell when they start
That soon there's a knife in their heart
Addiction's the name
And I have the blame
For murder: a hideous art

Often many people say yes
When they're all in their fancy dress
'Cause, sure, they'll be fine
Just a small glass of wine
Then without it, they start to stress

It's a traditional thing
For soldiers, the queen used to bring
People smoke and smoke
Until they choke
To the cigarettes they now cling

It was just a simple dare
'Take a pill, it's only fair!'
Addiction started
Became cold-hearted
A look became a crazy glare

Only downloaded an app
Though life would be gone in a snap
That comment was bitter

Wait! What's new on Twitter?
No mention that this was a trap

No matter the size of the cause
Once you walk through the doors
You can't get out
You'll scream and shout
Until you find a chainsaw

So before you start something new
Before any trouble can brew
Think, don't get addicted
Or like I've predicted
Suicide will come and find you...

Heather Dunsmore (11)
Ash Manor School, Aldershot

A Sporty Tale

Sport is everywhere, it brings us all together
Inside and outside, whatever the weather
But it can also disappoint and divide
When we can win or lose in the blink of an eye.

Sport can lift you up to achieve great things
It can take you as high as a bird with wings
But if you lose it can feel like a fall
And make your dreams seem very small.

Sport can improve your life and your health
At the top of a game it can add to your wealth
But it can also injure and make you ill
You can get disappointed and lose your will.

Sport can disappoint and yes you may not always win
And you may have to take defeat on the chin
But not to try and to ultimately fail
Is to miss the point of this sporty tale.

William Wedgwood (11)
Ash Manor School, Aldershot

Listening

Listening, it's important
If you listen you can get a job and make a living
To start, your mum and dad
They help you in life, they help you for school
They give you food and a bed to sleep in

Now your teachers, you may think they're annoying and mean
But you learn from them
You do your SATs in primary and you do your GCSEs in secondary
A levels in college and degrees in university

If you don't listen you can't get a job or make a living
No food, no home, no bed
If you don't listen at school you can't do your SATs in primary
Your GCSEs in secondary, A levels in college and degrees in university
So listen. It's important.

Kai Jepson (12)
Ash Manor School, Aldershot

Why The World Is Wrong

Bang! Crash! Smash!
Why is the world so wrong?
All we do is fight, kill and assassinate -
But why do we do it?
Why do we murder for pleasure?
No one knows why the world is wrong
Guns, bombs, bullets and knives are many methods to kill
Why do we do it?
World wars, political crisis, world hero assassinations and city bombing
Why so wrong?
There's so much prejudice such as racism, sexism, terrorism and schism
So wrong, just why so wrong?
Many people die, many people are born
But this global violence changes nothing
Stand out to violence and try smiling -
Maybe the world will change
There is only one way to find out!

William Fanthorpe (11)
Ash Manor School, Aldershot

Different

Joe told his son that it was fine to judge someone because of their looks
Or what they believe
So Jack thought it was OK
So he got his knife and stuffed it into his rucksack
He went out and saw a black person walking down the street
He stabbed him viciously
He put all his power into that one hit

People down the street
Watched him fall to his feet
Too afraid to do something
So what did they do?

Nothing

The knife in his back
Left a big hack
Innocent people left to die
On the cobblestones of that one street
On one day
That one person
Left to die just for the way they look.

Holly Andrews (11)
Ash Manor School, Aldershot

Flowers (The Meaning Of Life!)

Life to me is like a flower, every petal for every hour
Every petal that is picked off means an hour's gone, have you done enough?
Well, do not fear, do not worry, you've still got time, you don't need to hurry
But do hurry if you have a phone
As when you get older you will moan that social media is a waste of time
And that you could have been writing a poem or a rhyme
Or you could have been out there singing a song
Making you famous
If that's what you want
So it doesn't matter if your petals are dark or bright
Just get yourself out there and enjoy your life.

Tyler Lyons (11)
Ash Manor School, Aldershot

The Presidential Race

President. The top position
Donald Trump will surely cause demolition
He wants a wall
So no Mexicans, none at all
If Trump is a hater
Will the Americas pay later?
Trump will be in a grump
If he is not in front

Hilary Clinton
Could she be the first female president?
This will surely set a precedent!
She has beaten many others
And captured the hearts of mothers
They shout, 'You can win Hilary!'
But people ask, 'Does she have the ability?'
Will it be Carter, Regan, Bush then Clinton
Or will Trump win?
What's your opinion?

Oliver Hamer (12)
Ash Manor School, Aldershot

Education

Here I am
Sitting in a safe classroom
Without worry
Of being killed
As I sit here
With all of my friends near
I think of girls our age
Girls whose countries believe
That just because they're girls
They should not have the same human rights as boys
Girls who have to be scared of leaving for school
Every day
Just because of their gender
Just because they're girls
As I think, I realise
How privileged we are to be safe
And I decide
That I want things to change
Will it make the world better?
There's only one way to find out.

Maddy Williams (11)
Ash Manor School, Aldershot

Where Is The Justice And Law?

Where is the justice and law?
When people are dying in war
Leaders get richer with greed
When there are children that people can't feed
Families have no choice to flee
When we complain about the refugees
Their rafts sail as they come near
We look at them and snigger and sneer
But what is it that we all fear?
It's help that's why they come here
For miles they struggle and roam
One day they hope to go home
So I ask you to please understand
Reach out a helping hand
Show them what life is for
Where there is justice and law.

Emily Rose (11)
Ash Manor School, Aldershot

Women's Rights

Women are not machines
They need to be respected in our society, as men are
We must treat our mothers, sisters and daughters in equal measure
With our fathers, brothers and sons

We will all work towards a day, when women are complete equals to men in our society
I'm a woman and I am very proud!
The more power and equality woman have in our world
The less wars mankind will create
We have made great strides in the last century
Through the hard work, passionate behaviour and integrity shown by many women.

Chloe Evans (11)
Ash Manor School, Aldershot

School

Strange place school
Good but strange
For education, for friends
But it gets boring
As boring as watching grass grow
Still it gives you a life
If you have a dream you have hope
It gives an education
That's boring
It gives you friends
That's fun
But what's the point of having friends when you can't talk to them
If you have an education
You can have a good job
If you have a good job, you can fulfil your dreams
Think about this
What if the world had no schools?
You decide.

Alfie Drake (11)
Ash Manor School, Aldershot

Racism

Racism is around us everywhere
For many people are living in despair
Many can be black or white
And for them, life might not be as bright
We see the sad colour of racism not every other day
But every minute of the day
Racism, racism, racism

Many people hold up their flags
And many enjoy going around to brag
Thousands of individuals going through discrimination
Maybe even while on vacation
Is it right to day such things?
For everyone shall spread their wings
Racism, racism, racism.

Swasti Sharma (11)
Ash Manor School, Aldershot

Food

Food is nice and tasty
Food is good and squishy
It has a texture that's so yummy
It fills up the whole of my tummy

Different tastes and chewiness too
But if you eat too much you have to go to the loo
Food is so nice you could call it scrumptious
And it's totally delumptious

All different types like dairy and protein
They're all so nice but keep your hands clean
If you don't cook food properly
Then you won't be alive and that's a warning from me.

Daniel Westcott (12)
Ash Manor School, Aldershot

Life Or Death...

You could feel it coming
Didn't know what, but knew it was there
Waiting
Waiting to pounce
To kick you down when you're low
To push you to the ground
When you're weak
You know it was there but
You didn't know what
It makes you angry
Want to fight it
Makes you sad
Want to light it, fight it, spite it
It would go one of two ways
Give up, take it, death
Fight it, defeat it
Live
You knew I was there
But you didn't know what.

Liona Platford (11)
Ash Manor School, Aldershot

Failure

Sick of the same days
The repeating days
The 24/7 set up

Telling me I'm a failure
Grown-ups and my parents
Keep instilling confined dreams to me

'A score does not define who you are'
I lie to myself again
It hides the truth and tears me apart

Never mind
Like I said before
Don't worry about me

I can have a taste of frustration
Also irritation
And still bow my head in the end.

Khushi Limbu (13)
Ash Manor School, Aldershot

Stop!

Stop!
We have to think
Nobody is the same so just *stop*
We might look the same, but we are not
Everyone is different

Stop!
We have to know
Different values, beliefs, wants and needs
Determine who we are, so *please*
Treat us different

Stop!
We have to remember
That colour, religion, gender and race
Can be put aside and the person embraced
Judge us different.

Daniel Bunce (11)
Ash Manor School, Aldershot

Questions?

Why do people commit crime in such a sneaky way?
What's happening in the big world?
With deforestation and terrorists, what will save our Earth?
How many people want to start World War III?
How much more murderous madness could the world take?
Will we be wiped off the face of the Earth?
So many questions can be made
But how many can be answered without a doubt?
And that's all the world is now
Nothing good, just a doubt, a question mark.

Alexander Stephen Turner (11)
Ash Manor School, Aldershot

Autumn

Autumn is a time when leaves
Fall of the trees

As cold nights have begun
Morning frost will come

Food is gathered on a mountain steep
So animals can start their deep, deep sleep

Big, small, they fall to the ground
Brown and dry they blow around

Walking through the crushing of leaves
Whilst I shiver in the cold autumn breeze.

Daniel Hebberd (12)
Ash Manor School, Aldershot

Every Star!

Every star is a lifetime
You'd better make it count
Every star will fade
As your lifetime comes to an end

So never waste your star
As your life might be short
You never know
Until you go
What your life meant

Your star will be with you
As you grow older
Your star will fade
So make your star count
And don't be ashamed.

Hollie Eaton (12)
Ash Manor School, Aldershot

The Long Begotten World

There is a world out there
Somewhere for us to pray
A world of colour and light
Full of great might

Animals from a far-off age
Turning over the next page
The exotic leaves fall to the ground
One by one counting every pound

Yet I sit on the bed
And look out the window with my great head
If only I could touch it
The long begotten world.

Niamh McFadden (12)
Ash Manor School, Aldershot

We Are Responsible

If the trees could speak
Oh, I wonder what would they say?
Creatures strong but weak
Relieved to live another day

People scream in pain
While others bawl in victory
Really, what did we gain
From watching others' misery?

We are responsible
Both good and bad
But tell me, is it possible to think of
The life that someone never had?

Sian Gillingham (13)
Ash Manor School, Aldershot

Animal Cruelty

Winning, shaking, boneless
That was Stanley
He was beaten and left for dead
Would you like it to be done to you?
Scarred for life
Animal cruelty is rife
Abandoned in a ditch
Left by a witch
Strung up by string
Can never block out that sting
Is it alright to be starved?
It's not right to always be nerved
Would you like that to be done to you?

Jess Peacock (11)
Ash Manor School, Aldershot

Rights

Girls have rights
They're not all right
They don't really care
They aren't fair
Girls try to fight
For better rights
They try hard
But can't get far
Stay at home they say
Why is it us who have to pay?
Men don't realise
We have feelings
They hurt us
Discriminate us
They think we are OK with it
But we are not.

Sasha Marie Garratt (12)
Ash Manor School, Aldershot

I Am An Ickle Little Tree!

I am an ickle, little tree
I help you breathe you see
If you cut me down
You will surely see me frown
For I am an ickle, little tree
Please save me
And my family
Recycle the paper you use
Along with your bottles, cans and shoes
I am the home for many creatures
Cut us down, you will be told
By your teachers
For I am an ickle, little tree.

Courtney Sivyer (11)
Ash Manor School, Aldershot

Why All The Make-Up?

She wakes up every morning and looks in the mirror
Not happy by what she sees
She covers her face with make-up
She thinks it makes her look pretty
Foundation after foundation she hides
Concealer after concealer she hides
Why hide behind a make-up mask
It is not that much to ask
You are beautiful, one day you'll see
Look in a mirror and you will agree.

Leanne Matthews (11)
Ash Manor School, Aldershot

Friendship

The best of friends
Change your frown
Upside down
When you feel down

The best of friends
Will understand
All your little mishaps
And always lend a hand

The best of friends
Will listen
And never share a word

The best of friends
Are worth more than gold
Give all the love
A heart could hold.

Kristina Allyson Ecclefield-Walton (12)
Ash Manor School, Aldershot

Chocolate

I love chocolate bars
And Magic Stars
Melting in your mouth
Bubbling in your tummy
Chocolate is so yummy

Bar after bar
Coin after coin
White, dark or milk
The texture is like silk
I always eat my chocolate quick
In my opinion it's well sick
It's so good I wanna dab!
That's why I think chocolate's fab!

Cerys Trafford (11)
Ash Manor School, Aldershot

Peace

Tonight I sit and pray
That tomorrow will be a better day
A day when there is peace
The violence, it will cease

Peace will win and fear will lose
It's your decision, you can choose
Search your soul, do what's right
Then there will be no more fright

Tonight I sit and pray
That tomorrow will be a better day.

Niamh Wilson (11)
Ash Manor School, Aldershot

Poetry

Tick, tock, tick, tock
Clocks doing their job
Overseers staring at our papers
Pens eyeing at the paper
Minds go blank
I sigh
Time goes on
People scribble frantically
It's a race against time
I pick up my pen and move my hand
I draw
I can draw many things
But with poetry
I can master greater things.

Billy Dong (13)
Ash Manor School, Aldershot

Identity Theft Crisis

Identity theft is a big problem
And there isn't enough ways to solve 'em
If someone doesn't catch them
Something might start to happen
Maybe war?
And who for?
No one
And the rights for some
Though I am not a victim
And not so many have been
I am stating that it's a *major* crime
... For the time.

Iosto Iacomelli (11)
Ash Manor School, Aldershot

Bullying

Bullying is a thing
You cannot fix
When others around you
Won't let you mix

I never saw this coming
What's happening to me?
Why won't these bullies
Just let me be?

Feeling so upset
Feeling really uptight
I was born to learn and
Not to fight.

Emma Chapman (11)
Ash Manor School, Aldershot

Nature

Nature may hurt
Nature may make you cry
But it keeps the planet alive
Thriving and spectacular

It has been around for millions of years
But we may lose it in a mere hundred

So protect, help
And keep it safe
From that nasty race of destruction.

Joshua Lytton (11)
Ash Manor School, Aldershot

A Phase...

I don't know how this happens...
Best friends, drift away and then... nothing
Little girls with big hearts that hold even bigger dreams of their friendship, really holding together...
A bond so strong
Where nothing could go wrong
Right?
This then kick-starts a roller coaster, which runs on the strings of your heart and emotions
You cannot truly figure out if they really care
You then rely on their emotions
Does their face light up like it used to, when you walk into the room
Or do they barely notice you?
Casting you into the darkness
The shadow of your 'everlasting' friendship
Where you are left with a feeling of emptiness
Craving their presence
Their existence
Their friendship
'I'll be there till the end!' they said
Like every best friend would
But quite often I wonder...
Were they ever there in the first place?

Freya Eve Kinlough (13)
Bridgemary School, Gosport

Through My Eyes!

Through my eyes, the world is definitely different!
Sometimes, the lonely world to you is a land of no worries to me
I see the world in a unique way
Who knows if the sea is green or blue?
Nobody does

The colours of the rainbow: red, yellow, pink, green
Purple, orange and blue
Is this just a statement that everyone is being forced to believe?
Fascination...

Fascination is the word people use when we are aesthetically amused by someone or something
For instance, take your favourite flower
Are those daises white or blue?

What if primary school colour lessons shape the way children see things
Our minds could be tricked by this!
This makes our perception the same...

When the skies are grey, some people feel blue - but not me
I feel yellow because I view everything with a smile!

Why are feelings always associated with colours? Be different
Make yellow your angry colour and pink your shade of elation

What everyone sees in black and white, I see in vivid colour
Why are blondes always deemed as 'dumb'
Be the bright blonde that outshines everyone else
Don't follow stereotypes

The world is your canvas, so use it
You are as free as an eagle in our land of gazillions
Break those ridiculous laws of society
Be different. Put on the glasses of life and rock them!

Hannah Graham (13)
Bridgemary School, Gosport

You Feel...

You look at this image and you feel powerless
You see the traumatised, delicate eyes gazing into
Your soul, asking for help and your body is overcome
With emotion

You look at this image and you feel angry that an
Innocent little boy has been caught in the political
Game of war that haunts his precious mind - that will
Eventually become his nightmares

You look at this image and you feel a great cloud of sadness
Hang over you, the blood trickling down his face is like a
river
As it meets the cuts on his neck - when did children deserve
This pain?

You look at this image and you just want to cry out - what
Did humanity do to deserve this? Most kids never see
anything
As life-changing as this little boy did - he saw people die
before
His eyes and yet that to him is normal

You look at this image and you feel the dust covering
His body, cover yours, it makes you feel dirty and
claustrophobic
But to him he feels this every day - just today he's been
Noticed by the world

You look at this image and you think, *Where have I seen this?*
You've seen it on the front cover of all the newspapers in the World but this is just one in millions of children in the same situation
On the brink of death...

Liberty Kappa (14)
Bridgemary School, Gosport

Nothing Is Impossible

The season is drawing near once more
On the first drive I know we'll get a score!
I managed to defy the selection pattern
Little old me! How could that happen?

Training was strenuous this year, but no one wanted to yield
We just wanted to be back on the field!
How long would we have to wait?
To start the party at the Tail-Gate

The coach journey was very quiet
The team wouldn't deny it
They then slowed to a halt outside the ground
The noise from the fans was an incredible sound

As we walked out, the atmosphere hit the team
We could hear the supporters start to scream
The air became electric
The ball soaring through the air was just majestic

Now was our time to shine
We won't put our season on the line!
Our leader brought up to the line
I knew then it was *my* time to shine

The ball was thrown to me
Running to meet it I had never felt so pleased!
I was going to reach the end zone!
Six points for me!

The game was ours, it was finally done
We had only gone and won!
1 and 0, onwards and upwards we go
Now let's go to the Super Bowl!

Luke Tunstall (14)
Bridgemary School, Gosport

Life Poem

What is the meaning of life?
Us being on this world, but what's the point of it?
What's the point of society today?
Wars minor and major
Sexism
Politics
The list goes on
Do you think that we're just made up of atoms and molecules
We breathe until we die
Or is it something on a bigger scale?
Like we're made to make a difference
To change things
Has it ever occurred, no matter what your life brings, someone on the other side of the world has no idea who you are or what your story is?
In all honesty, I'm inferior
I'm not going to change the world or make a difference
There are people doing better
There's someone prettier, smarter or changing the world
So back to society, let's think:
Bullying
Peer pressure
Racism
So again, what's the meaning of life?
Is it to do good; strive to be better?

Or to get on with life and hope for the best?
All these questions over a life
I don't think there is a meaning to life
I think if I disappeared tomorrow the universe wouldn't really notice
So maybe we're not living anymore, just surviving...

Crystal Frampton (14)
Bridgemary School, Gosport

'...I Really Like Greek Myths...'

The Greeks gave us mythology
That engraved the brave into astrology
They gave us deities and extreme power
Who ruled upon us from their mountain tower
From the luck of Tyche
To the bittersweet embrace of Aphrodite
And the endless darkness of Nyx
To the destructive force of the River Styx
Along came the inventor Deadalus
The all-powerful Tartarus
The titan lord Kronos
And the everlasting Chaos
To the well-known Heracles
From the ominous Erinyes
The fearless Atalanta
The goddess Hestia
And the mighty Perseus
Jason and the crew of the Argo
The twins Artemis and Apollo
Flying high to the Pegasus
Shuffling along with the Empousai
The grim, morbid service of Charon
Great leaders taught by Chiron
Hundreds of gods
Thousands of creatures
With snake hair and heads of dogs

Tales of strong, noble heroines and heroes
Who threw accurate spear throws
Who led lives of misery and hate
Caused by the intricate weaving of the fates
Teaching valuable lessons that beat like a drum
Sharing their world for millennia to come.

Livia Giles (14)
Bridgemary School, Gosport

Athletics!

The butterflies in my stomach
Won't go away
Neither will my shaky legs
But today is the day

I've spent all this time training
I can't let us down
Because we want to be
The greatest team around

The gunman gets ready
My heart starts to race
300 metres seems so far
But I'll set the pace

Bang! The gun is blown
Everybody sprints off fast
But if I stick to the pace
Then hopefully I won't come last

But, they're all so quick
So I have to up my game
Keep my legs moving
And stay in my lane

As we come round the bend
The finish line's in sight
The crowd are going wild
Because I've got the gold tonight!

Hannah Childs (14)
Bridgemary School, Gosport

Mercy Or Genocide

The peak of the mountain that covers me is called Mount Ebott
Dark as the words as the flower speaks to me
I thank whatever patience may be for my unconquerable soul

In the fell clutch of Asreil I did not fight but had mercy and integrity.

Under the piercing of my knife, I leave a trail of dust everywhere I go
Whereas some others may have kindness

Beyond this place of extreme anger and tears, looms justice of the dancer and scientist
And yet the terror of ages, will find me, with bravery.

It matters not how much I bake, how charged with perseverance you must show.

I am the master of my fate: I am the captain of my soul
You are filled with determination after reading the poem.

Brett Reynolds-James (11)
Bridgemary School, Gosport

Photograph

The key to a thousand memories
Two seconds to take, virtually impossible to erase
Capturing the moment when everything is just perfect
Even if that's just a second
It lives on forever
Immortal

People, places permanently etched into our memories from the press of a button
Relationships remembered purely by the joyful smiles and happiness beaming through the image
A portrait of the times we've shared, both good times and bad
Documented forever in our hearts
Immortal

All this emotion, pain or joy, heartbreak and betrayal or elation
Held in a second, frozen forever
Immortal

Nothing can be forgotten, that's what I love about photographs.

Serena Jane Day (13)
Bridgemary School, Gosport

War

War must be stopped
A violent bloodbath of wrong and right
As the bombs are dropped
Innocent souls turn off their lights

The soldiers grind at each other
Their bodies dropping every second
Tears falling for distant mothers
This should be stopped - I reckon

World leaders gaze at what they have created
This Great War
These maniacs are hated
As the planes soar

This cannot be mended
And neither will the scars
For the fields which we once tended
Are now factories for cars

This cruel act needs to end
Never to happen again
Why can't we all be friends?
It will happen - but when?

Harvey Ayling (13)
Bridgemary School, Gosport

Untitled

You can feel the rush of blood
As you run across the field
Moving in the veins like blood
You know in your heart that you cannot yield

Together they worked like a machine
There was a prospect - a chance of winning
As long as they worked as a team
They would finish the match grinning

I couldn't stop as I ran and ran
I couldn't disappoint the cheering fans
I knew in my heart that there was a plan
If I did my part it would be grand

The ball flew like a bullet from the throw
As I caught the ball and thought, Go...

Jack McEwan (14)
Bridgemary School, Gosport

Poem About Reading/Writing

Opening the book to a whole new world
Lots of things can happen every day
It's like living in your own dreamworld
But it would have to end some other day

It could be about anything you want
Like unicorns that can poop rainbows
It could even be about a plant
That could live in a grassy meadow

Your ideas are never-ending
Like a queue to the girl's bathroom
Lots of people like to spend time reading
You could even do it in the store room

But all stories have to end
Sometimes they never have to end...

Millie Edney (14)
Bridgemary School, Gosport

Untitled

Abandoned apartment, I look and glare
While lost souls are screaming throughout the air
I cautiously walk across the old, demolished grounds
Stepping over graves surrounding their commander's bounds
Colossal trees stand before my eyes
Guarding their master's secrets and lies
One bright light gleams at me
Telling me to come in and see
As dark as the midnight sky, the sky gleams and does glow
The heavy statues hold the house from below
The misty sky covers the house
Stopping me from looking in!

Keira Garrett (11)
Bridgemary School, Gosport

Sleep

Silver slivers slide through the curtain gap
Shining on my warm cosy pillow
The bed is illuminated by the shimmering light
Waiting for me to crawl in
Streetlights outside, forgotten about
As I drift away to Dreamland
Colours fill my mind
Swirls and wonderlands
Mystical creatures run wild alongside me
Hours, which feel like minutes, pass
Sunrays pour through the curtain gap
Burning brightly against my closed lids
Tiredly I push back the covers
Getting up ready to start another day.

Callie Moore (15)
Bridgemary School, Gosport

It's Scary

I sit in the dark
And concentrate on the pain of his mark
It's scary

He picks me up and spins me round
I hit the rock-hard ground
It's scary

I feel the touch of his knuckle
Him and all of his friends chuckle
It's scary

His words scar my heart
The words all over my art
It's scary

He can't hurt me anymore
It ended in gore
It's scary

Don't bully
It ruins lives.

Lewis Walker (14)
Bridgemary School, Gosport

Poem About War

War is hell
For all that fell
For the people who were writing
To the many who were fighting
Food was scarce
For the people who were scared
The poppies are there
To remind you we care
They are red to remind us of the dead
Who now lay in a box-shaped bed
Horror, terror and tragedy
Left sorrow in the minds of the families
Of the many soldiers who now lay dead
To allow us to sleep comfortable in beds.

Tyrone Martin-Menditta (13)
Bridgemary School, Gosport

Life

Life:
Life is like a camera, just focus on what's important and capture the good times
Develop from the negatives
And if things don't work out, take another shot

Death:
Because I could not stop for death
He kindly stopped for me
The carriage held but just ourselves and immortality

Wolves:
Lone Wolf I be, Lone Wolf
That's me, Lone Wolf
I'll die
No one will cry.

Lee Brown (15)
Bridgemary School, Gosport

The Competition

The feeling before you step onto the mat
Is almost like a panic attack
You practise all year round
Hoping your stunts don't fall to the ground
Other teams you hope to destroy
Let big, sparkly bows shine with joy
Jump higher than everyone else
And I
Eat - sleep - drink
Cheer!

Ellie Moore (12)
Bridgemary School, Gosport

My Phone

Parents don't understand
Why we have this gadget in our hands
It's almost like it's superglued
Without it we don't know what to do
Would you put your phone away?
That's what they always say
Parents just don't see
Without my phone - I'm just not me!

Rhys Lewis (12)
Bridgemary School, Gosport

Food

Food is love
Food is life
Food is what I crave at night
Sneaking downstairs for a treat
Hoping and praying there's something to eat
But the fridge is empty
The cupboards are bare
I stand there staring... gasping for air.

Sommer Moore (14)
Bridgemary School, Gosport

Regret

Sitting in the dying grass
Amidst a field of broken glass
Looking up at the sky
Wishing he could fly
Away, away
To the dawn of a better day.

Rowan Males (16)
Brockwood Park School, Alresford

My Imagination

I imagine in the mornings
I imagine at night
I look and gaze to the wonder of life
I pick up my pen; I sit at my desk
Starting slowly
Colours start to emerge from the tips of my pen and out of my head;
They join and create a wonderful pattern

What could it be?
Van Gogh's yellow paint, forming the yellow house
Or
Georgia O'Keeffe's pink and blue musical art
Or
Mary Cassatt's pretty purple in a pot of purple flowers?
What could it be?

It turns out that it is your imagination flowing
And the wonders and powers that you can make
Just by using your imagination
Your imagination.

Yasmin Sirokh (11)
Charter Academy, Southsea

Mischief Managed

My obsession with Harry Potter
Is getting a bit ridikulus
It's getting out of hand
I wave my magic wand
In Harry Potter's land

I give Dobby a sock
And suddenly he's free
The Marauders would have
Done the same for me
Moony, Wormtail, Padfoot, Prongs
Were always there for me
When Voldemort was set to kill me

My parents let me escape
But they ended up getting killed
Hagrid found me and Sirius came too
I would have to live with the
Dursleys and my evil cousin too

Padfoot is my godfather
Moony is my teacher
Wormtail is a traitor and
Prongs died for me.

Sabrina Victoria Robson Thompson (12)
Charter Academy, Southsea

At Home

At home
Where nobody is known
The clock starts to ring
Tick-tock, tick-tock
The tap starts dripping
Drip, drip, drip

At home
Where nobody is known
The wind starts blowing through the window
Whoosheeeesoooo, whooooshheeeeooo
The lights switches off and on
Che, cho, che, cho

At home
Where nobody is known
The cat starts miaowing
Miaow, miaow, miaow
The dog starts barking
Ruff, ruff, ruff

At home
Where nobody is known
Who could it be home
A ghost
A demon
Who!

Haseena Rahimi (11)
Charter Academy, Southsea

Truth

Life is not the perfect picture you see
You have to go through pain, believe me
Like whenever you feel fat or ugly
It's all about the images you see
On the TV or magazines
Looks like they have the perfect life
But behind that page or TV screen
You see what their life is really like
The tears and the dramas
Because they're just like you and me
But is life all about your image
Or is it about your personality
Whether you're kind, caring and loving
Or vain, perfect and shallow
I think life is about your friends and family.

Poppy Edwards (13)
Charter Academy, Southsea

A Christmas Day...

Christmas is the time for laughter and cheer
Adults enjoy a glass of wine or beer
You can hear the carols being sung from far and near
The snow is cold and making people shiver from ear to ear
Stockings are being hung by the fireplace
Children are awaiting Father Christmas with haste
When they awake there will be presents under the tree
There will not be one child present-free
We all sit down for dinner with our Christmas hats upon our heads
After a fun-filled day we are ready to rest our heads on our beds.

Lily Drennan (12)
Charter Academy, Southsea

Memories Kept 'Til The End

I wait every day for night to fall
Because I want to see a beam of light
Shining from the sky so bright
It reminds me of my family who I've lost
But when I look back down
I see someone there to comfort me
We think of the happy times that once covered our minds
But eventually we realised we will see them again
I see a picture on the wall with my family at Christmas
Enjoying time together
We all love, care and adore each other
But one day my head will be forever left to rest with my family.

Jack Drennan (12)
Charter Academy, Southsea

The Man In The Park

He was walking through the park
On a warm summer's day
When a dog started to bark
He had nothing to say

When he got home
He had a little groan
Suddenly, he had to pick up the phone

He had to keep his tone down
There was a baby upstairs
So he went into town
And cut his hair
To relieve his stress of his everyday life

Frankie Wall isn't very tall
He likes to drawl
As he is a fool
When he sits in the pool.

Frankie Wall (12)
Charter Academy, Southsea

Sing From The Heart

Sitting, thinking, dreaming, waiting
Is it all that I've been anticipating?
To stand before a sea of faces
And release the words locked in my heart

Unleashing all that may consume me
This is what my future may be
Shaky hands, cold shivers, slipping down my spine
I stand behind the curtains...

Finally my moment has begun
The dam has fallen and the tide has come
I step out to the brightest spotlight
Start to sing and lose my fright.

Jasmine Alicia Smith (13)
Charter Academy, Southsea

My Childhood Nan

You left me here
But I sense you're near
You watch me from up above
With your heart filled with love
Why'd you leave me so early
I was only a little girly
Nan, I miss you
When you helped me put on my tiny shoes
You would pat my head
As you sent me to bed
You gave me Chewits
Each time that you'd visit
But now I feel so cold
As I grow old
You're in my heart
Wherever you are
I miss you.

Natasha Spree-Ashdown (13)
Charter Academy, Southsea

Computer Programming

Computer challenges ahead
Over-complicated puzzles
Mini marvellous macros
Programming in python
Universal understanding
Tricky in learning
Easy to master
Ready for progress
Pie is simple
Running to class
Over many stairs
Going up the floor
Really is annoying
A class that I like
Many things to do
Must continue on
In the classroom
Never giving up
Go to be a computer programmer.

Dylan Wilding (12)
Charter Academy, Southsea

You Are The Person

You are the person who ties me up
You are the person who bosses me about
You are the person who leaves me there
You are the person who leaves me nothing
There's a person who strolls by
There's a person who rescues me
There's a person who cares for me
There's a person who keeps me safe
There's a person who took me in
A place I can call home
A person I can trust.

Daisy-Nell Tupper (12)
Charter Academy, Southsea

The Owl

Glowing eyes stare silently at you
Curled with a pointed tip beak waiting to
Snap! Snap! Snap!
Multicoloured feathers camouflage in the night
Super sonic ears listen for its dinner
Powerful wings spread out like an aeroplane
Dagger-like feet grab ready to pounce
Gliding like a mythical monster
Waiting to swoop
Waiting, waiting
Attack!

Christopher Barker (11)
Charter Academy, Southsea

Untitled

Travelling through the time
You see all sorts of crime
Daleks and time lords
Give terror to the worlds
Dr Who, where are you?
Save our world, time is running out
The TARDIS is big and blue and looks like a police box
Hurling through the black hole into various locations
Can the doctor save our planet
Or will we be exterminated?

Ethan Newton (12)
Charter Academy, Southsea

Music Is Marvellous

Music is marvellous
It makes me feel good
It makes me feel happy
The way that it should

When I listen to music
It makes me feel free
Like a bird taking off
On the flight of destiny

Music is marvellous
It fills me with love
Like a bird spreads its wings
My spirit takes off...

Humayra Elme Ali (12)
Charter Academy, Southsea

Cold Day Poem

There's no sun today
Just a grey sky
As the wind blows
It feels so cold
As you walk to school
Frowny faces covered the walls
Tap tap the rain goes
Whoosh, whoosh the wind blows
So stop a minute and smile
Lighten up this nasty day
Let the sun shine
Through the branches
I say!

Hana Tvardkova (12)
Charter Academy, Southsea

When I Was A Child

When I was a child
You made me smile
Even when I was down

You made me laugh
You made me giggle
Even when I had a frown

You made me cry
In my darkest times
And you made me down

And that's the thing
I love about you.

Poppy Cartwright (11)
Charter Academy, Southsea

Her

A dead soul that was screaming for revival
A young girl who became suicidal
There were kicks and hits from society
That's probably the reason that I suffer from anxiety
Death threats every time I logged in
Damn, here we go again
I was pretty much alone, always looking for new friends
But that didn't happen so here I am wishing it would end
But it won't, it never will, there'll always be something
Every time I felt good then they would remind me, was nothing
Every time I felt down they couldn't help themselves but enjoy it
It tears me apart, takes all the fight that I have left in me
But maybe now that it's just modern day society
I had enough so I decided to run
Away from all this drama and to stop them having fun
But I can't run forever, eventually I'll get tired
So I just stare at the rope and hope my my life will expire
But they still wonder why she cuts
As she picked up the blade
She thought her scars would never fade.

Robyn Langston (13)
Regents Park Community College, Southampton

Free Love

We grew up in a world
Where free love is restricted

Seeing boys together
But my mum said they shouldn't
Walking down the street
In which two girls began to kiss
Raised my head to look at Mum
As my dad frowned and hissed

Though that was never the end
They spun me around
Buried my head in their chest
And whispered to one another
How gays should be buried to rest
Implying that gays should not be allowed to live
And they took life for granted
Through what God has to give

'Girls should be with boys
Gays are nothing but toys.'
They will soon fight back
Using a powerful voice

We are all unique people
With likes and dislikes
Dark to pale skin tones
With all equal rights

Suddenly
The news was breaking
On my TV screen
It starts flashing

People, homosexuals
Shot, dead and gone
What have they done?
That is somebody's son
A beloved child
Killed with two deadly guns
Gone too soon are their precious lives

Dear people who murdered
How did you feel?
Anger, shock or guilt?
As identical crimson blood
Made a bloodbath appear

Appearing like a sea
Now what do you see?

Multiple broken families
An ocean of tears

And a mother
One father
Very much like mine
However mine would grimace
What an obvious sign

'Oh no, gays are near
They aren't like us
They're way too queer.'

But
Now being lesbian, gay, bi
Genderfluid, hetro or pan
Is now of equal rights

Though some can still not accept
That homo and hetro
People of the same sex
Are now free of restriction
Most countries have legalised
Free love has permission

This world escaped from humanity
Drove until all traces of freedom
Was completely gone

Thankfully we have regained all the love
With a heartfelt song

What is it called?
Where is the love?
Purify all hearts
Purer than a white dove

Fortunately we have it back
Here is the love.

Heaven-Leigh Monces (14)
Regents Park Community College, Southampton

Trapped

Imagine a world where everyone was sad
Not because of low phone battery,
But the loss of humanity

A world were no one wants to be part of the community
Because they're trapped in a screen

No time to daydream

But time to blog, type, vlog, Skype
Nothing better than Facebook, Twitter, Instagram
Nothing worse than online scams

A world where posting is a sport and commenting is an exercise
Being photographed from birth to when you die

You can't autocorrect who you want to be,
That's what life's for figuring out

We need to turn behind our shoulder
Escape the video game
Look behind the camera lens and capture these moments
But not with our phones, with our minds

Rather than joining a wired world
We need to disconnect -

And then reconnect with the real one.

Edie Smith (14)
Regents Park Community College, Southampton

My Bullying Poem

All those voices shouting, laughing, because no one will care
Telling me I'm wrong, telling me I'm stupid
To change my awful clothes, to change my horrible hair

They're all laughing at my shape, pointing out my fat
fingers, fat toes, my rounded stomach, my rounded nose

They taunt and jaunt as they're sneering
Picking me apart bit by bit while the rest are cheering

They back me into a corner whilst they're having their fun
I have no will to fight and no strength to run

As quick as a flash! I fall to the floor
I feel as if no one else will ever see me
As if the people surrounding me make a very good door

Someone help, the voices are screaming now
I try to escape from them, but I don't know how
They're towering now, drowning me
Pushing me out of existence
Pushing me down, surrounding me

I scream, I scream, I scream, I scream
Scared and angry, questioning any judge
How these people are supreme

The voices are getting quieter now
I know my brain must be dying now
Everything's going to mush and I'm crying now

A soft voice, a kind smile, a pair of arms surround me now...
I think it's the end of my story now...
Or maybe it's just the start...

Aimee Hollie-Jean Cartmel (13)
Regents Park Community College, Southampton

The Bumblebee

Fly little bumblebee, fly, fly away
Let the wind brush its gentle fingers past
Your delicate bumblebee wings of pure
Transparency, as you fly yourself back

To your bumblebee honeycomb hive in
The low down branches of the treetops
Where you lay your sleepy head at night
And hum to yourself a bumblebee lullaby

Dream, just dream about the pollen,
The nectar and the honey
The honey is your baby, in texture it
Is runny

Pollinating flowers to help keep our
World alive, you try your best little bumblebee
To work away your worries and our worries too

You help us when we are sad and when we are blue
And bring my garden to life
As you spread your magic dust upon the flowers and
They dance in their beds to the

Melodic tune of the bumblebee's buzzing
Remember the bumblebee and his black and yellow back
Where he carries his pollen
Just like Santa and his toy sack

Treat the bumblebee well
For he is as peaceful as a dove
With the bumblebee around

The world is full of love.

Isabella Richardson (13)
Regents Park Community College, Southampton

All I Want Is You

A game between me and you
Who will win and who will lose?

The world gets involved
Will the puzzle eventually get solved
Will I be hurt in the end?

The future is a mystery
Will our love become history?
It's all playing in my head

You play me like a controller
Do you still talk to her?
Never mind, I'll just cry instead

I feel like I'm a new game of FIFA
I get kicked around the pitch
The one to end up with a stitch
On my forehead
My mum's friends on the other end
All worried except you

It all started back in Year 7
Hoping to last till Year 11
I miss the old you
Is there a button to undo?

Can I have you back
Instead of an ice pack
Just to be together
In the cold winter weather
To cuddle and keep warm
And keep me safe from the storm?
Love takes two
Just me and you.

Mia Breedon (14)
Regents Park Community College, Southampton

Depression

I'm afraid to say I'm losing
You either win or die trying
Depression is a war
I think I might surrender
The constant battle with myself
There is no escape
There is no light
I think I might die a little more tonight
It's a never-ending struggle
The never-ending pain
It's like I'm going a little bit insane
It's a bottomless pit
Filled with a sea of emotions
You can never be saved
You're always drowning
You're afraid of living
You wake up into Hell
You look in the mirror
You just stare for a moment
And see the monster you are
People don't talk to you
They see the scars
And they knew the addiction
You overdose

They release it all for you to put it back in your body
They let you out with a bit of therapy
And yet I'm still left with a bit of death inside me.

Olivia Ebbutt (15)
Regents Park Community College, Southampton

Never Give Up

The world of sports is very big
From the football, rugby and boxing
If it's a try, a goal or a home run
It will bring you closer to a victory

When you play football
It's always a struggle
But if you try you will always come by
Pacing down the wing
Cross in the box
And score an overhead kick
Goal! 90 minutes is up
Making you closer to the cup

When you do boxing
You may not play well
But never give up
Surge through the pain
Fight! Fight! Fight till he is down
Don't give up until you push through
Put down the gloves
But only if you never give up

We live in a world of sports
Don't give up until you succeed
Whatever you do, live the dream up
Famous or not, quite even if you get let down
Don't stop trying until you cannot play any more.

Luke Day (13)
Regents Park Community College, Southampton

Abyss

Dearest one, hearest thou my voice still?
Search the abyss of thine heart
To find the passion hidden in the deep darkness.

Dearest one, hearest thou my voice still?
Search the Earth,
Search the seas,
Search the skies,
As left alone dearest one thee would only suffer and hate thyself...

Dearest one, hearest thou my voice still?
Search until you find the true and only,
The light to thy darkness,
The sun to fill thy void before thee is too late.

Dearest one, hearest thou my voice still?
If thy passion is not found,
If thy abyss has spread,
And thee forsook all hope
Then look to the sky and await thy rest.

Dearest one, hearest thou my voice still?
Dearest one?

Patryk Mikietinski (15)
Regents Park Community College, Southampton

Suicide

Social media is always a drain
People type, they put things in your brain
You're ugly, you're worthless, it's always the same
They never realise that you're in pain
You try to make yourself stronger
They bully you longer, you feel nothing will change
It leads to addiction
It's always addition, changing your dose, it's a range
You start thinking about it all
You become suicidal, laying drowsy in your bed
You say you can't do it, the people try to change it
But you're hooked on the voices in your head
You find a quiet spot
To make it all stop
This is the time to say goodbye
You pick up the pills
It gives you the chills
With the last breath, you're finally still.

Jaymie Stevens (15)
Regents Park Community College, Southampton

Kipper

Oh Kipper, what a friend you were
With your pointy ears and wiry fur
Your playful nature shone right through
When playing with your toys you loved to chew

You loved your walks
You would set the pace
We'd remind you, 'Kipper! It's not a race.'
And how we'd laugh when time was up
You'd turn into a stubborn pup!

You talked to us through thoughtful eyes
And sometimes deep and meaningful sighs
You loved to chill out on your bed
And rest your happy, handsome head

Oh Kipper, what a friend you were
With you pointy ears and wiry fur
But now you're tired, it's time to rest
Goodnight, sleep tight, you're Heaven-blessed.

Nathan Hill (13)
Regents Park Community College, Southampton

Seasons

Seasons, there are four seasons
Summer, autumn, spring and winter
All these seasons are so good
All these seasons are different
There are summer, autumn, spring and winter

The first season is summer
Summer makes me very happy
In summer we feel very hot
Go to beaches, ice creams
New dress and rainbow

The second season is spring
We are very happy
New clothes, new flowers
We all like spring

The third season is autumn
We feel small and cold
Because the next season is winter
No leaves, no flowers like that

The last seasons is winter
So happy because it's Christmas
Snow, new dress, new coats
We feel very cold.

Mishel Mathew (14)
Regents Park Community College, Southampton

Families

A connection by blood
But not all the time
They can be bound by love
A connection that is deep
A special link between parents and children

In them -
We share a special relationship
Yet sometimes they can break
We share our achievements
Yet sometimes they are not really important
We share our thoughts
Yet sometimes they're heartache
We share our problems
Yet we usually hide it
We share our disappointment
Yet sometimes we conceal it

The beauty of family is imperfect
Like everything isn't perfect
But sometimes
Being perfect is what it is
To be a family
All you need
Is love to bind us all.

Emily Grace Fraser (13)
Regents Park Community College, Southampton

Molly

There once was a girl called Molly
Who was shopping with her mother
Whilst sitting in a trolley
And making rude faces at the people passing by.

What a naughty girl was Molly
To make faces at the people passing by
And every time her mother looked at her
She would give her a massive sigh.

As they turned the corner to pick up some fruit
Molly threw the things out of the trolley
'Oh, what a naughty girl you are
To throw the things out of the trolley'.

When they got to the cashier
And put the fruit and veg on the belt
An old lady smiled at Molly
And the little girl smiled back and it made her mother melt.

Malika Chentoufi (13)
Regents Park Community College, Southampton

Christmas

The best time of the year is Christmas
Christmas is the time to put up a tree and make it look pretty
Christmas is the time to watch a classic Christmas movie
Christmas is the time to share gifts and Christmas cheer
Christmas is the time to count down to the best 24 hours of the day
Christmas is the time to wrap up warm with hat and scarves
Christmas is the time to play in the snow and fight with snowballs
Christmas is the time to get the best food and chocolate
Christmas is the time to spend with family and friends and the people who love you
Christmas is the time to make amazing memories to cherish forever
And that is why Christmas is the best time of year.

Angel Freeman (14)
Regents Park Community College, Southampton

Snowflake, Snowflake

I woke up this morning to see that you're here
Snowflake, snowflake, I've been waiting all year

Autumn is over and the leaves have turned to mush
Snowflake, snowflake, get ready for the Christmas rush

Swiftly, gently, you fall to the ground
Snowflake, snowflake, you don't make a sound

Snow is piling up to my knees
Snowflake, snowflake, I'm getting a cold and I'm starting to sneeze

Your crystal body starts to shine and glisten
Snowflake, snowflake, you must listen

To the bells, chimes and Christmas cheer
Snowflake, snowflake, Santa Claus is nearly here!

Madi Bennett (13)
Regents Park Community College, Southampton

Panic

It overwhelms, consumes, eats and chews
It cares nothing about you
Whenever, wherever, however it pleases
It cares nothing about you!
It breaks, shapes and brings you down
It cares nothing about you!
It brings shaking, sweating, blood and tears
It really does care nothing about you
It's an anxiety driven feeling where there is no control
It makes you want to run for the hills, or crawl in a hole
Hold tight, be strong, stay calm, don't run
For it's all in the mind, it feels real
But no it's not!
So the next time the adrenaline releases into your veins
Stay seated, clear you mind
You can do it - game on!

Alisha Danielle Hooper (15)
Regents Park Community College, Southampton

Nice Evening

It was supposed to be a nice evening
The sun set in the pale blue sky

Clusters of people crowded around the road
A familiar midnight-black dress came into view
Her chocolate-brown ringlets matted with blood

It can't be her; crimson blood oozing out
The sounds of whispers vibrated my ears
Ambulance lights blaring

It felt like hours waiting in the bland hospital room
Nurses and doctors walk past
It was nearly midnight
I still remember the four white walls trapping me in

The rest of it was a blur
But I keep replaying that night
It was supposed be a nice evening.

Cora Byrne (13)
Regents Park Community College, Southampton

The Family Situation

When you go home hearing your mum cry
You say, 'Mum, why you crying...?'
She says, 'Your nana's passed away with cancer...'
You just start thinking about all the memories in your head
And start to cry out
This makes you think about all the good things
She's my inspiration because she was the one who acted like God
Controlling all the family
But as she fades away people who were close to us don't really care
Because of all the favours we used to do for them... they are moving on
It's not the same any more
My words are spitting out as if it's over and out
It has all backfired now...

Ajit Digwa (15)
Regents Park Community College, Southampton

Time Stood Still

As time stood still Sandra knew
She knew all hope had been abolished
Time had run out
Faith had been lost

Darkness had taken over
Sandra was lost in a sea of tears
Shaped by the despair that ruled over her
Lost in the depths of her thoughts

The moon calls her to her darkened world
She's been welcomed with pain
Pain that's dragged her down
Pain that's built her up

Suffering makes her stronger
Sorrow gives her hope
Fear gives her power
But life makes her victorious.

Evelyn Lexie Pybus (13)
Regents Park Community College, Southampton

Pray, Cry And Give

Finding, searching... what have they done wrong?
They have been struck by bombs
No food, no water, no house to live
Crying their eyes out for their parents to breathe
Like a tumbling tear, they cry out their fear
With no parents to care
No one but 1,000 people are dying every day
Do we notice?
Their future is like a cloak of darkness
Having hope they'll live
Pray, try and give
That's all we can do
Have hope for them
That's all we can do
What have they done wrong?

Minshana Muneer (14)
Regents Park Community College, Southampton

A Broken Family

I knew this would happen from the very start
How dare you do this to my family?
You tore us all apart
Look at my mum, she's crying on the floor with her broken heart
Now a year has gone and you both have properly part

Now the divorce papers are through!
And I don't care about you
You've ruined everything
You're trouble, trouble, trouble

And the saddest thing comes creeping in
That you never loved me
Or mum or anyone or anything.

Phoebe Harris (13)
Regents Park Community College, Southampton

Good Girl, Bad Boy

Good girl, bad boy
That's how it always goes
Everyone knows I like him
Even he knows

I sit at home wondering
Wondering why...
Knowing it wouldn't work
So I sit there and cry

Walking into school
His eyes pierce into mine
I look down and walk away
Hearing a faint sigh

Our paths cross again
He leans in for a kiss
As we pull away he whispers
'I've been waiting for this.'

Szarida Ciwinska (13)
Regents Park Community College, Southampton

Everyone Is Different...

Everyone is different
No one is the same
You just need to treat
Everyone with respect

No one should be left behind
Everyone deserves a chance to shine
No one should be left behind
To fail and throw it all away

Don't you throw this away
This decides your future
So think
Work hard
And succeed
So think
Work hard
And succeed
This is your moment
Don't let anyone stop you.

Jake Barry (14)
Regents Park Community College, Southampton

Equal And The Same

All the same
In the world full of hate
Judged, demonic, feared
All because of different beliefs
It's not just them!
Our looks, language and culture
We are judged in the world of hate
Different, but all the same
But don't worry, it's just them
People who are dreadful and dire
They will break you...
It's okay, because one day
They will understand
That we are all equal and the same.

Aleksandra Koperkiewicz (15)
Regents Park Community College, Southampton

Family

Sometimes mums and dad fall out of love
Sometimes two sisters are better than one
Something you can't tell your father, cos he thinks you're too young
He won't understand... teenager stuff!
Sometimes family live too far away
Sometimes you feel the need to just run away
Some things you have to sacrifice
To be able to be nice
Cos it's your family, at the end of the day!

Robyn Caine (13)
Regents Park Community College, Southampton

Winter

Snow is falling
Everywhere I look
I'd love to cuddle up with a hot chocolate
And read my favourite book
However I can't because I've finished my favourite book
But don't worry...
I'll be getting a new one for Christmas

How mysterious
Imagine seeing Santa on Christmas Eve
How fun would that be?
That would be like the best winter for me!

Emily McLachlan (13)
Regents Park Community College, Southampton

Kick About

Going out for a kick about
Packing my bag, gotta go out
Scoring from the penalty spot
While my sister does a dot to dot

Dribbling past the opposite team
Hopefully, I follow my dream
Passing through them like there's no one there
They're just giving me the stare.

Sam Bowyer (13)
Regents Park Community College, Southampton

American Money

Money's as green as grass
Money is dead presidents
My money runs in my pocket
Money tracks me down
Messing with money is like messing with the monster
My money: big, green and long
My money is my life
Cha-ching
Too much money can kill you!

Ajaypal Singh (13)
Regents Park Community College, Southampton

How To Meme 101

Roses are red
Violence is bad
Harambe was shot
And that was sad

Roses were red
Violets were blue
I have crippling depression
And so do you

Roses are red
Balloons are blue
The killer clowns
Are after you.

Liam Kennedy (14)
Regents Park Community College, Southampton

The Legendary Night

It surrounds us, an imitating army dressed in black,
The keeper of skies: moon, is their eye as bright as a cat's?
Its laser-like beams scan its home,
Peeking through the hollow gaps as it moaned.
As it stares with a grin upon its face,
It is always seen all over the place.
The creatures wriggle out of the curdling soil,
As their injured prey limp away skin in oil.
The houses are a border separating the city,
Nobody can come in, the people find it a pity.
The houses depressed eyes glow in the dark,
It can be seen in the vivacious park.
The swift shadow slipped through the preternatural park,
The lumbering figure teetered on his late-night lark.
The gnarled branches twisted pointing at it,
As if on cue the sky was strangely lit.
The thick mist crawled into its place,
As the azure troops poured to base.
The truth is threaded through the lies,
Unpick the needle.

Stephane Yonga (14)
St George Catholic College, Southampton

Mums

Mums, the lifesaver of the day
The treasure that holds you
Tight
They do so much for you
As she did
For me

She held me tight when
I was one
And helped me walk
When I was two

She stopped all the screaming
Tantrums
When I was three
And walked me to school
When I was four

And took me on a ride
When I was five
She bought me a gift
When I was six

She took me abroad
When I was seven
She gave me a piece of cake
When I was eight

She read a rhyme
When I was nine
She took me on a plane
When I was ten

She said, 'Everything will
Be OK,'
When I was eleven

But sadly, she is gone
Now
I won't see her
Again
However, at least I know
She'll be
In my heart forever.

Olivia Wakely (11)
St George Catholic College, Southampton

I Want It! (Stealing)

Have you ever
Seen something you want forever
Telling people you have that already
But you don't and you have to stay steady?

See something in the shop
It is your favourite top
You open your purse and all you have is five pounds
The top costs twenty-five pounds

What are you going to do?
Are you thinking what I'm thinking too?
No, no stealing - it is fine
But look, it is stealing in my eyes

You walk in the store
You want to walk more
But no, don't do it
Yes, you should do it

You grab it
Stuff it
Run for it
Feel guilt for it

I did something wrong
You have nightmares for so long
Please learn not to steal
Learn from me not to do it - or you can't ever finish your meal.

Yulu Chen (12)
St George Catholic College, Southampton

Equal Rights

I am a person
We are all people
At least I thought
Before the battle began

They say I am different
They shout and they scream
But I am who I am
At least that's what I thought
Yes, that's what I thought before the battle began

I am cast out to the deepest depths of my heart
Left to drown in my own tears
I thought we were all human
Our differences were celebrated
But that's what I thought
Before the battle began

But that is all behind me
My sorrow gave me strength
I'm not second, I'm first
I'm not different, I'm unique
I don't know inequality.

Oluwatitofunmi Euler-Ajayi (11)
St George Catholic College, Southampton

Why?

Here, there and everywhere
I see a look, then a stare
I try to ignore more and more
But this isn't right, I'm sure.

So what if I am not the same as you?
Nothing's the same - a baa isn't a moo!
So why do you stare yet ignore me?
Why do you walk away instead of talking to me?

I'm a human like you
Touch me - I'm real
What's the big deal?
I have dreams too...

I want to fly, to spread my wings
I dream about what happiness brings
But at the moment - I'm tied down
I wear on my face one huge frown...

No one deserves to be ignored.

Erin Brady (11)
St George Catholic College, Southampton

War

Why?
We had to flee
For no one but us could hear our desperate cries of agony

Death
Heart pounding, blood bleeding we attempted to escape the never-ending battlefield
Enclosed in the walls of war, we've been sentenced to death by our own people

War
Shell-shocked, we migrate across the sea
But this is just as dangerous as where we came from

25 left yet only five live
This will surely be the end for me
Waiting, waiting, waiting for land
Yet another wall has prevented us from safety

We keep dying one by one
Yet war keeps going, it goes on and on.

Martin Shumba Mulenga (12)
St George Catholic College, Southampton

Save The Environment

Environment is important
Treat it with respect
Please do not neglect
Don't leave litter on the floor
Would you like to know a bit more?
Pollution will harm the outside space
The underwater world is a beautiful place
Throwing rubbish into the sea
Will make the water green like a pea
The rain helps plants grow
And the sun gives a bright glow
Plastic, paper, glass and tin
Must be thrown in your recycling bin!
Chopping down trees will affect animals
They will growl and howl like cannibals
It will make them die
That will make me cry!
Reduce, reuse, recycle!

Natalia Spyt (11)
St George Catholic College, Southampton

Here Is A Poem About People

Here is a poem about people
People who are all different
Shapes and sizes, white or black
Fat or thin, tall or short
Everyone is the same and that
Is what everyone should think
People may bully, people may laugh
But I think that people
Should be treated like any other person
People may get things right
People may get things wrong
But people start to get bullied for things
That are not their fault
I try and stand up for people
But they never listen to what I have to say
This is a poem about people
People who are all the same.

Molly Barker (11)
St George Catholic College, Southampton

Emotions

Happiness is key, but sometimes sadness is mean
It can blow your inside and tear your outside
Anger can get your fist moving but kindness can make your hand shaking
But sometimes the world can turn you blue
Blue as the Mediterranean Sea

Fear can prevent but curiosity can inspire
It can inspire the choices of life
Jealousy is big but it can be a secret if you're jealous of your friend's amazing rhythms
Emotion is the king of all those feelings
But try to encourage all the positive ones.

Daniel Hamidy (11)
St George Catholic College, Southampton

Racism

People think an average person is white
They say this is right
This is why I wrote this poem
So I can show 'em
That they are wrong
Black people are not made for songs
To discriminate
So why is there so much hate
Don't they deserve a normal life
Not to be hit with a knife?
They were not made to do the dishes
They are here to succeed missions in life
So stop with the racism
And give them a life without criticism.

Mehrab Choudhury (11)
St George Catholic College, Southampton

Hate

Hate... Hunger... Society
Every day, every hour, every minute, each second
For those starving this day, ditched, neglected
The language, words of pain, which souls absorb; all the same
Offence, jealousy and large egos
Actions that kill friendship, feeling and all
Unfair rules, completely unequal, less income, authority and food
Why oh why the racism, sexism and religious discrimination?

Philip Wilk (11)
St George Catholic College, Southampton

Inequality

Inequality kills people, why
Don't people share
Equality should be over the top of bad things
The Queen should stop this
Unfairness is eating people
A lot of people
People have to fight against this
The idea if this is breaking my heart
Trouble is the only word that I can say about this
You could be the one that changes the world for better.

Wiktoria Krupa (11)
St George Catholic College, Southampton

War Zone!

War zone
Where birds have never flown

Bad guys and good guys
Where one dream dies

Hate and negativity
No place for sensitivity

Justice and equality
Not a policy

Immigrants and delinquents
Stay or go, still with consequences

Yes or no
They still go

Elections.

Michalina Wielgosz (11)
St George Catholic College, Southampton

Equality...

Equality...
Short or tall
Black or white
Doesn't matter whether you are liked
Friends or not
Don't lose the plot
Because someone is still with you
Female or male, have faith, so... help us have equal rights!
Old or young
Nothing is impossible
As long as you use your heart
Then you can believe to achieve.

Ethan Marston (11) & Ellie
St George Catholic College, Southampton

Crime Is Not A Laughing Matter

C rime is an offence, it doesn't make you look big or hard, if you have

R espect you will stop because it's harmful, the economy survival will be

I mpossible, you have to stop, this is real life, it's getting out of control, you can't

M anoeuvre out of this one so stop and

E njoy every day.

Luke Hooper (11)
St George Catholic College, Southampton

Spotlight

Black or white, no need to fight
We're all different
That's what makes us brilliant
Nelson Mandela wouldn't stop
So why now make the economy drop?
Society is high
Don't make black people want to die
Everyone deserves equal rights
Let's all have a bit of spotlight.

Jowan Healey (11)
St George Catholic College, Southampton

The Shadows From Behind

Everywhere you look, darkness comes out
The sun falls derelict like shadows
All you see is the moon glowing
So you know darkness is here...
Never go out or darkness will follow
You from behind in the shadows
You turn around, nothing
Shut your curtains and don't look!

Roman Allen (11)
St George Catholic College, Southampton

Hatred

H atred kills innocent people that want love and happiness
A llows to eat your heart
T alk to people about it, don't let it take you
R uthless is hatred
E motions are happy, not sad
D on't treat anyone how you don't want to be treated.

Daniel Sebastian Koch (11)
St George Catholic College, Southampton

The Falcon

As it swoops down and up, moving its wings freely through the snowy Alps
Losing concentration by doing loop-the-loops
Soaring through the sky were the planes from Zurich
Locked on radar for Munich
Now the falcon swoops down low
As it knows it's not far from home.

Charlie Wright (11)
St George Catholic College, Southampton

Jealousy

J ealousy ruins our lives
E ven over our friends
A nother one ends
L oving stops
O nly real people can
U nderstand what
S cars people for life
Y ou'll get jealous sometimes, we all do.

Abi Ogunleye (11)
St George Catholic College, Southampton

Hope

Trees rest for hundreds of years
Cut down for supplies
Until the day there is no more

  H ope stays clearly in our hearts
  O thers may say it is just fantasy, but
  P eace will happen until
  E veryone has hope.

Dann Lacea (11)
St George Catholic College, Southampton

Justice!

J ustice
U nites everyone
S top being the bad side of you, regret
T reating people badly
I f you don't want to be the one
C reating hatred in the world
E veryone needs justice!

Akbar Majid (11)
St George Catholic College, Southampton

Image

Nobody looks the same
We are all different
Personality, looks or colour
However it doesn't make a difference

Just because we look different
Doesn't mean we are different
Only personality separates us.

Zhiyong You (11)
St George Catholic College, Southampton

Image

I mage, it doesn't matter what you look like
M asses of people get
A ffected by this
G ross feeling
E veryone is different
If we were all the same
It would be boring.

Olivia Proud (11)
St George Catholic College, Southampton

Peace

P eace is what we want
E quality is key
A nother person starts crying because their life's destroyed
C harity is waiting
E verybody has a chance.

Samuel O'Callaghan (11)
St George Catholic College, Southampton

Tick-Tock

I'm staring at my watch.
The seconds are ticking by,
Tick-tock,
One, two, three
That is three seconds of my life gone.

I'm sitting down and watching TV,
In thirty minutes I must make a decision,
I know it's not about precision,
But it's got to be a vision.
Tick-tock,
One, two, three
That was thirty minutes of my life wasted.

Thinking that I can see the future,
I wonder where I would be in a few years time,
But it's just a matter of time,
Tick-tock,
One, two, three
And I'm still staring at my watch.

Landing Badjie (15)
The Connaught School, Aldershot

Alone

Alone.
Scared and worried.
Lost and confused.
My mask is firmly on my face.
Laughing my life away to force back the tears.
It's funny how people see nothing but my mask.
I never realised just how pointless life truly is.
No matter what you do,
No matter what you say,
No matter whether or not you want to,
In the end, you just...
Disappear.
I feel so pointless,
Though I know not, want not to give in
to the sweet release of death
In fear of everything falling apart.
But, in the end,
We will all be forgotten
As nature continues its cruel and vicious cycle,
Until one day, everything ends,
And existence is no more.
All that keeps me going is my family,
In a world where I want to go home,
But I am not sure whether or not I belong at this place I call home.
So someone please, hear this poem and change your heart.

Do not be the type of person who makes someone feel lost,
Be the type of person who finds them and helps them,
In order to slowly change this heartless world of war and injustice
Into one of peace and love.
Hear my words and end your pain,
Make this world loving again.
In all these times of war and strife,
Be the one to save a life.

Nicholas Jarrett
The Connaught School, Aldershot

Penelope

Dear Mummy,
I'm now 4. Daddy says you're in Heaven now - I hope you're okay.
I've just started infant school. My teacher is really nice.
Not all the girls are nice to me but that's okay because my teacher plays with me.
I've learnt how to count up to 20 and am top of my class.
Daddy's really sad without you though, I hear him cry sometimes at night after I've gone to bed.
Lots of love
Penelope xxx

Dear Mummy,
I'm now 7. Daddy says you're an angel! Are you my angel?
I've started junior school and I've met this boy called Jack. He's my best friend.
We play with each other all the time; he even sometimes comes round after school to play.
His favourite colour is green - just like me!
Daddy is still really sad and cries all the time.
Lots of love
Penelope xxx

Dear Mummy,
I'm 13. Daddy says you look down on us, is that true?
I've started secondary school; I'm in Year 9 and still best friends with Jack.
I miss you. Every day something new happens that I know you would love.

Jack is funny, but we always get in to trouble at school for talking in class.
Daddy doesn't really talk to me anymore.
Lots of love
Penelope xxx

Dear Mummy,
I'm 17. Daddy says you can walk on clouds! How cool is that!
I got As and Bs in my GCSE but mainly As! I'm starting college soon - wish me luck!
Jack and I have started dating! Weird, right?
Jack makes me laugh when I cry and happy when I'm sad - he's a keeper.
Daddy goes out a lot and shouts at me.
Lots of love
Penelope xxx

Dear Mummy,
I'm 24. Daddy says you're dead and that I should stop writing these letters.
Jack and I are getting married soon - I can't wait!
I picked out my dress and everything. It's so pretty!
The wedding will be beautiful and I wish you could be there.
Daddy's gone now. I don't see him any more.
I hope you're okay.
Lots of love
Penelope xxx

Dear Annie,
Don't worry. I'll take care of Penelope.
Love Jack x

Isabella Stapley
The Portsmouth Academy, Portsmouth

Untitled

Bully, bully, bullies
They push me to the floor,
And slam me to a door.
Each word,
Each name,
Each touch makes me feel like a game. I'm just a piece in the play.
I'm letting them win; I don't want to be a piece in play.
I go home each night cry and lie to all that want to know what's wrong.
I look down at my phone:
You're ugly
You liar
Kill yourself;
I don't cry any more, I just sit and stare into the darkness of my mind.
The words take over me I just want them to be kind.
I don't know what I did for people to treat me like this.
I don't think I'm made for this.
I tell myself, 'I will try again tomorrow'
But I have given up with trying.
The knife in my hand and their voices in my head telling me to end.
It's time to end this game.
I've held this down for too long, it's time for me to go down with the rain.
Goodbye and I hope you're good being queen.

Rheanna North (14)
The Portsmouth Academy, Portsmouth

The Day In The Life Of A School Pupil

I wake up and dread the day even before I get changed.
Change, change... this word is so strange.
I head to school, my face growing longer.
Longer, longer, longer...

I get to school, head to my usual place,
A place where no one can see my face.
My looks show that my life's in disarray,
My face displays my complete dismay.

The lessons feel so slow - my heart races faster,
Faster and faster, my work's a disaster.
All I can focus on are the voices from behind,
Saying things that are not kind.

The day's almost over, but I must go through lunch.
The school bell summons the horrible bunch.
Bruises on my skin to add to my collection,
The main reason I wear make-up - bruise colour correction.
It's the end of the day and it's time to go home,
But I don't go home all alone.
I walk, then I jog, then I begin to run.
I sprint so fast because if I don't I'm done.

The teachers at my school don't even care,
They don't touch the subject, they don't even give it a glare.

It turns to night and I cry myself to sleep.
These events will always repeat.

This is the day of the life of a student and her abuse.
In situations like these, it's themselves that the victims will accuse.
They always hide the fact that they're insecure,
But just asking if they're OK can be a cure.
This poem is meant to give bully victims a voice,
So people like them can gain back their life choice!

Lilly-Rose Adams (13)
The Portsmouth Academy, Portsmouth

Illness

She's been waiting in the back of
an ambulance for quite a while but
finally gets through the door.
With beds in the corridor - nowhere to go,
it's not looking too good for her.

One hour has passed, finally.
The chaos has stopped. Waiting
for the doctor to examine her.
At last she goes off for a scan.

Later she returns in pain.
No one nears to kill the pain.
Assisting others, not killing the pain.

Sending her home because
she 'looks' too well. Doesn't mean,
she is well. Waiting to be discharged but
going home is what she wants to do.

Two hours later, she is rushed back in.
Why did they discharge her? Being put on a drip.
She not a number, she's got a name!
They only want the bed for another.

Later she returns in pain.
No one nears to kill the pain.
Assisting others, not killing the pain.

Chanice Stevens
The Portsmouth Academy, Portsmouth

You Just Have To Wait

Stuck in a world,
A world where no one likes you.
Where your best friend is your knife,
And you constantly want to end your life.

A world where your only escape,
Is to drag a blade across your wrist.
Where you say 'I'm fine',
But you mean 'I just want to give up'.

You lie to your family,
You are forced to hide your wrists.
You're afraid to go to school,
Just because they say you're not 'cool'.

Stuck in a world,
A world where you're on your own.
You don't feel safe in your home,
You live in fear.

But there is hope,
You just have to wait.
Find that person,
It's up to fate.

Kya Athena Patrick (14)
The Portsmouth Academy, Portsmouth

Smile. Laughter.

It has been said that if you smile you'll get wrinkles around your eyes.
If you laugh you'll get wrinkles around your mouth,
These are called laughter lines!
But they are the best wrinkles you can get.
When I'm older I hope I have wrinkles around my mouth and eyes because that would've meant that I've had a happy life full of laughter.
If you don't smile, then smile because scowling and being mad all the time gives you the wrong type of wrinkles.
Laughter lines are a sign of beauty to people who believe in true happiness.
I like being happy.
Do you?

Kitty Lydford
The Portsmouth Academy, Portsmouth

Depression And Anxiety

A big black monster with glowing red eyes
never lets you out of your own home.
You can't leave or you'll panic -
Stay at home!
Stay here.

The monster has a friend.
That monster makes me sad,
makes me feel like dying...
Always alone.
You have nobody.

Stop!
I don't what this!
I want them to leave!
They are not friendly monsters
They're not you or me.
They are depression and anxiety -
The monsters many fear.

But it's OK- don't worry,
Your friends are always here.

Macy-Mae Jenkins (13)
The Portsmouth Academy, Portsmouth

Love Poem

Love can hurt,
When someone breaks your heart,
They act like they love you,
But they tear you apart,
They say I'm sorry,
But they never mean it,
They make me worry and make me cry,
It's like I'm a joke,
And not even there,
They find someone better,
And say bye-bye,
It hurts you inside,
That you're not the one,
They find someone else better to go and have fun,
They say they'll be here till the end,
And say they'll be your best ever friend,
Or maybe more than just a friend.

Tasnim Ahmed (13)
The Portsmouth Academy, Portsmouth

Dad

I miss you. The day you left it felt surreal.
All I have is memories.
I can't remember your face.
I can't remember your voice.
I have pictures but none of them help.
I need you.
All I think about is what you'll miss.
Growing up without you will forever haunt me.
I'll always remember you.
I will never forget you.
You'll always be with me.
I love you.
I miss you.
I will never accept that you're gone.
You're shining bright in the sky.
You light my heart up every night.

Caitlin-Rose Goode
The Portsmouth Academy, Portsmouth

Bad Hair Day

You think you're having a bad day...
Bad hair day you call it...
But my day started off fine
But then I got the news... what news I hear you ask?
Cancer, chemo
And my hair would disintegrate
I would have no hair!
Now that is what you call a bad hair day
Each day my hair would fall on the floor
And I would look at in devastation
And another part of me disappeared
Don't take your hair for granted.

Mia Marner (14)
The Portsmouth Academy, Portsmouth

Pandas Are Not Endangered Anymore

The giant panda's past has been horrifically relentless
Hunted by poachers they were left defenceless
Deforestation took over their lives, by getting rid of their bamboo supply
Their soft fur is taken to make clothes for locals
Leaving them cold and lonely whilst in the horrific captivity
People are leaving them neglected and abandoned
It is not their fault that they have no purpose; or do they?
One day these mystical creatures could be extinct - but wait, a miracle has happened... but now their lives are not saddened as...
Pandas are no longer endangered
Which is tremendous
Their numbers have increased by a huge amount
By people giving donations and as being a symbol of WWF for many years are finally being free from captivity
They are cute and cuddly, also soft and important in Chinese society
Loads of people are inspired by them and they have been treasured and special for many years
Love them and save them and make them feel part of your heart
Have hope for these adorable creatures
Will you be destined to keep these huggable, lovable creatures and fulfil their future of freedom?

Chloe Headland (15)
Wildern School, Southampton

Hurricane Matthew

Crash!
The sound of children filled the city
Bare trees do the cha cha
Police, fire engines, ambulance sirens go off
This is all because of Matthew the hurricane

In houses families cuddle up
They can hear the wind whistling through empty streets
Rubbish from bins roll around uncontrollably
Everyone petrified for their life
It seems like everything in the world is going to die
All because of Matthew the hurricane

Everything stops in the world
The sound of children crying their eyes out stops
You cannot even hear the people breathe
Crash!
The stupid hurricane Matthew

Bins are rolling over in the street
The wind picks up
Dogs howl, cats miaow
Young children screaming at the top of their lungs
The hurricane is destroying everything
Will it ever stop?

Madeline Bendell (11)
Wildern School, Southampton

A Sense Of Belonging

Lost. Abandoned. Unwanted
Cast out by the world around you
Where do you go?
When you know you can't be accepted
In a world of cruelty, war and inhumanity
How can you feel loved?
Yet love those who hate you?
But who would want to belong in this evil place?
Where you're endlessly judged
Religion, sexuality, gender, colour
Who cares?
Yet it seems it matters
It's the reason you're pushed away
The reason you will never fit in
And the reason you want to fit in
To be the same as everyone else
But maybe you're not, because
You are unique.

Esme Thompsett (12)
Wildern School, Southampton

Syria Crisis

The endless cries
Unending bloodlust
War.

The sound undying
The dead keep coming
War.

Everyone gone
To a shameless cause
War.

A saviour is needed
Will one ever come?
War.

The war continues
And many keep going
War.

Think to the future
Will there ever be one?
War.

We are meant to treasure
Protect our world
War.

I think to a day when this will all be over
Thinking again I can't imagine a world without it;

An unending war
The Syria crisis!

Elizabeth Pugh (11)
Wildern School, Southampton

Are We The Same?

Are we the same?
No
Should we be the same?
No
Is that a good thing?
Yes

Differences left, right and centre
Nothing and no one are the exact same
Not even apples born from the same tree
Especially not us, human beings

We are different in every way
This is a fact we cannot change
Being the exact same would not be fun
We would not be different

Are we unique?
Yes
Are we clones?
No
Are we insecure?
Yes
Are we the same?
No.

Victoria Anne de Bruijn (11)
Wildern School, Southampton

Animal Crisis

I know people say just walk away
From endangering animals and that's the way
From every day
'Cause the abuse ain't cute
Imagine if that was you

The fur from jaguars and tigers
You don't need it, you just wanna see it
Poor, defenceless creatures
At least that's how everyone should see it
Don't kill
Or steal their skin
Did they give you permission?
No, they didn't.

Tia Lucking (12)
Wildern School, Southampton

War

A landscape in an etched form.
Streaks of ash scraped across the intoxicated air,
like someone had spilt charcoal on their art piece.
Silhouettes creep through the deserted land, waiting for their world to shatter

The gun will fire soon enough,
Dating the wounded's fate.
And all that's left is no respect,
Just a name buried in soil.

Robyn Harfield (12)
Wildern School, Southampton

401 Marathon

Running for charity is so much fun
A marathon a day, what a run
Travelling over the country
Place to place

'Cause I'm beating everyone in this race
Southampton, London, Manchester
Bournemouth, Liverpool, Winchester
I'm winning them all
Because I'm the best runner of them all.

Mia Gregory (12)
Wildern School, Southampton

A Matter Of Life

170,000 left homeless
This is not just a story
But a matter of life

Diseased food and water
This is not just a problem
But a matter of life

The country of Haiti
Must stay strong
This is not just a fact
But a matter of life.

Katie Ridout (11)
Wildern School, Southampton

YOUNG WRITERS INFORMATION

We hope you have enjoyed reading this book – and that you will continue to in the coming years.

If you're a young adult who enjoys reading and creative writing, or the parent of an enthusiastic poet or story writer, do visit our website **www.youngwriters.co.uk.** Here you will find free competitions, workshops and games, as well as recommended reads, a poetry glossary and our blog.

If you would like to order further copies of this book, or any of our other titles, then please give us a call or visit **www.youngwriters.co.uk.**

Young Writers
Remus House
Coltsfoot Drive
Peterborough
PE2 9BF
(01733) 890066
info@youngwriters.co.uk